Let Every Heart Prepare

Meditations for Advent and Christmas

Barbara Cawthorne Crafton

MOREHOUSE PUBLISHING
HARRISBURG, PENNSYLVANIA

Morehouse Publishing
P.O. Box 1321
Harrisburg, PA 17105

Morehouse Publishing is a division of the Morehouse Group.

Hymn lyrics are from *The Hymnal 1982,* copyright 1985 by The Church Pension Fund.

Printed in the United States of America

Cover art: Kactus Foto, Santiago, Chile/SuperStock; *Mary and the Baby Jesus,* Ximena Cousino
Cover design by Trude Brummer

Crafton, Barbara Cawthorne.
    Let every heart prepare : meditations for Advent and Christmas / Barbara Cawthorne Crafton.
      p. cm.
    ISBN 0–8192–1755–7 (pbk.)
    1. Advent—Meditations. 2. Christmas—Meditations.   I. Title.
  BV40.C68
  242'.33—33dc21   98–27850
                                                                 CIP

To my brother,
David Cawthorne, 1948–1998
Your cat says hello.

Preface

A lot of people I know read two or three of these little meditation books at once—just a snippet of something to get them thinking in the morning, at lunchtime, or at night. Different people do different things as far as their spiritual routines are concerned and, in prayer as in panty hose, one size definitely does *not* fit all.

So use this book as you will, in whatever devotional pattern you have made your own, and enjoy. I hope that you find yourself humming familiar tunes to yourself as you read, and that the condition persists for the rest of the day. I can think of worse things to be haunted by than hymns.

My thanks to Church Publishing Incorporated for allowing our wonderful hymnal to be plundered for this effort. We are blessed in this book of poems set to music. Thanks also to all the people who worked so hard and so well to revise it twenty years ago or so, many of whom are still alive, though some have fallen asleep.

First Sunday of Advent

From human will you do not spring,
But from the Spirit of our God.

ATTRIB. AMBROSE OF MILAN (340–397); TRANS. CHARLES P. PRICE (B. 1920), HYMN 55

The Virgin Birth has fallen on hard times in recent decades—it has seemed to many women, and to some men, that emphasis on the virginity of Mary has put those of us who long ago abandoned that state at a disadvantage by comparison with her. And it is certainly true that the Church has often exhibited a horror of human sexuality that has done nobody any good and many people considerable harm.

But is squeamishness about sex really what the Virgin Birth is all about? There is evidence in Scripture that disagreement about its particulars has been around just about from the beginning—nobody knows exactly what Mary's medical condition was, and nobody ever will. But the fact that this birth was an interruption of the normal course of human history is something everyone has agreed on: The life of Jesus was not an ordinary life. It had an extraordinary impact on the world. In Christ, the mysterious domain of God crossed over into the predictable domain of human beings. The Virgin Birth was not the last time something happened involving the life of Jesus that was difficult to understand. Hard as it is to swallow, it is nothing compared with what we'll have to deal with come Easter morning, a few short months from now. Look on it as a little something by way of a warm-up.

We don't have our babies just the way Mary did. We are assured, though, that our entry into the larger life is just like Christ's, the firstborn of the new creation, of whom we are all little brothers and sisters. Life with Christ in eternity is a life that is not ruled by the linearity of our lives, a life that knows none of our sad limits. When it broke into our limited world, some adjustments were necessary—Joseph, for instance, had to make a big one. But stay tuned. There will be more.

Monday in Advent I

Lo! he comes, with clouds descending,
Once for our salvation slain.

CHARLES WESLEY (1707–1778), HYMN 57

Prior to the time of Jesus' earthly ministry, people loved to predict a dramatic ending to human history. Everybody was writing about it. Some of their writings survive in our Bible, in the Book of Daniel, for instance. The Messiah descending on clouds of glory was often part of it—armies streaming from the sky to finish off the oppressor and usher in the kingdom.

I know how they envisioned the clouds—not as the leaden clouds, portending snow or rain, that we see in the sky during winter, but as glorious clouds: clouds afire with the setting sun, shocking golds and pinks and silvers surrounding a scarlet orb just before it dips below the horizon for the night. Clouds look like fantastic mountains, like radiant and very solid cities. Their thick, billowy appearance makes it look like a few armies could easily stand upon them.

They look like that from a plane, too. I never tire of gazing at them when I fly, mile after mile through the white meadows. But the clouds I see as billows are far away; the clouds through which I am flying disappear as I pass through, revealed as nothing more than fog. All that majesty, all that apparent substance—it's only water vapor.

As it was, Jesus did not come on clouds at all. He came in poverty and some embarrassment, the child of poor parents who hadn't been married quite long enough. That's one of the reasons why so many people failed to recognize him: Most of the people who were alive when Jesus was did not think he was the Son of God. Most of them went on about their business as if nothing had happened.

You'd think that those who *did* recognize who he was would have known better, but they didn't: When they began to talk about his return at the end of time, they went right back to the clouds for inspiration. "Sure, he came in poverty and weakness this time," they told each other, "but just wait until he returns. You talk about clouds!"

In observing Jesus' first Advent, we prepare for the second one—that moment when everything will have been completed. "He will come again in glory," we say in our creed, "to judge both the living and the dead." Clouds? Armies? Is that what his glory will be like? The triumph of an ancient emperor, the grandiose power furniture of another age? Might not all that turn out to be nothing more than mist, once we are there? The first time around, nothing was as expected. What makes us think the second will be predictable?

Tuesday in Advent I

Hark! a thrilling voice is sounding: "Christ is nigh," it seems to say;
"Cast away the works of darkness, O ye children of the day."
LATIN, CA. 6TH CENTURY; TRANS. *HYMNS ANCIENT AND MODERN*, 1861, HYMN 59

Thrilling. By now, the stores have been festooned with tinsel and fake evergreen for what seems like forever, in a shopping season that began just after Halloween and has been old news for a while. I remember, though, when the secular preparation for Christmas *was* thrilling, or so it seemed to me. Thrilling, and a lot shorter, of course—but we were all much younger then.

At first, it seemed that the thrill could be bought. I was five, and every little girl in kindergarten wanted a Tiny Tears doll. It was said that she could cry real tears. She duly appeared under the tree on Christmas morning, smelling that wonderful new-doll smell that everyone who was a girl in the 1950s remembers. I was too little to grasp how the crying mechanism actually worked, though; I made a big mess with water in the bathroom sink, but Tiny Tears's plastic cheeks remained discouragingly dry. From too much washing, the shiny brown curls soon degenerated into unattractive, dull spikes, and a permanent gray smudge besmirched the end of her nose. I had little investment in Tiny Tears beyond her trumpeted crying skills, and I quickly lost interest in her. That was my first clue that creaturely thrills are ephemeral by nature.

Eventually, everything gets shopworn. Now, years later, my own hair is a little spiky, and parts of me don't work all that well. I have calculated that one-eighth of my husband's scalp is now exposed to the elements; I recently heard one of the grandchildren ask him what color his hair used to be. So we are shopworn, too. But that's the difference between people and toys: Those who love us don't base that love on our pretended perfections. Love renders us lovely. The glittery things that stores hope we will buy are all symbols of love, though they seem far removed from it—things we can give each other to show how much we care. The more expensive, the better is what the ads tell us. And yet, we know it is not so.

This time of year is all about love, and things are no substitute for it.

Wednesday in Advent 1

Creator of the stars of night, your people's everlasting light,
O Christ, Redeemer of us all, we pray you hear us when we call.
LATIN, 9TH CENTURY; VER. *HYMNAL 1940*, HYMN 60

I've lost track of the number of people who have told me something like, "I guess God is just too busy with important things to bother with my little troubles." Now, that's a kind gesture, letting the Almighty off the hook like that: God let my tragedy happen because he was just swamped with his important work. But is God really like that—one more overworked CEO?

What would it mean for God to "hear" us? Is a desirable outcome the only thing that would certify God's hearing in all our difficult situations? When we turn to God in desperation and then things don't go our way, does that mean God didn't hear? Or that he just didn't want to help?

I certainly don't know what makes things happen in this world, and I never met anybody else who did. But I do know what helps me in the midst of my great need. I need to know that my pain is not mine to carry all alone, and it helps me to know that God hears me, even if nothing in the situation changes for the better, or even if it gets a whole lot worse. From the people around me and from my God, I want the same thing: not magic, not an exemption from the realities of human history, but a loving understanding of what I'm going through. I don't really expect to be fixed. I just want to be heard.

The other side of being heard, though, is listening. After I've ranted and cried and told my truths, I can be still and listen. I can listen to the friend who has patiently listened to me; she may have a word that I need to hear, a word that helps my healing. And, if there is no one else around, if it is in silent prayer that I have cried out, I can be still and listen with my heart. Not with my mind—that's just the noise of me thinking. Just with my sore heart, all cried out. And God will speak. And my heart will hear.

"Sleepers, wake!" A voice astounds us,
The shout of rampart guards surrounds us:
"Awake, Jerusalem, arise!"

PHILIPP NICOLAI (1556–1608); TRANS. CARL P. DAW, JR. (B. 1944), HYMN 61

Sleep is the Holy Grail of middle age. We hit the ground running, swim upstream all day, cover all the bases all the time, leave home early, and get home late. Rocked to sleep by the motion of the late-night train, we are awakened by the conductor's surprisingly soft tap on our shoulder, and we gather our things and stumble out into the night. "Coffee, anyone?" someone asks at dinner. We all look uncomfortably around at the other diners to see if anyone else is going to indulge. "I know I'm going to hate myself," we say, as the lovely dark brew fills our cups. "Just a half a cup," we say, "No, no more, that's enough!" We, who used to be able to stay up all night if we had to study for an exam, *covet* sleep, daydreaming in the afternoon about how good it will feel to lie down. "What time did you get in last night?" I ask my daughter. "Oh, I don't know, three or four o'clock, I guess," she says and I am appalled. But I notice that even she has just about stopped staying out late on work nights. Even my child is getting older.

In the morning I awaken before it is light. I open one eye to locate the lurid green numerals on the radio: four in the morning. I think of the work I might do if I were to get up now, the essay or two I might write, or the half hour I could do on the treadmill. Unfinished tasks at the church pluck at my sleeve; I could get up and do something about some of them, I suppose. But the bed is warm and soft; I pull the covers up to my chin and listen to my inert husband's regular breathing. Soon, my own becomes slow and soft, too, and sleep steals back over me. Just a little longer. All the things I have on my plate that need doing do not outweigh my longing for more sleep.

If Christ were to come now, to throw back the covers of my life, cuddled down in the comfortable predictability of its days, exposing me to the bracing air of a new day, it would be hard to respond gracefully at first. *Not now. I'm sleep-deprived.* But the sleep of the night is only for the sake of the day. God gives us the rest we need, and we need to take it. And then God astounds us with something new, and we awaken to it, refreshed.

Friday in Advent 1

***Zion hears the watchmen singing; her heart with joyful hope is springing,
She wakes and hurries through the night.***

PHILIPP NICOLAI (1556–1608); TRANS. CARL P. DAW, JR. (B. 1944), HYMN 61

No rendezvous is at too late of an hour or too inconvenient a place when one is in love. We sit through movies that bore us, football games we would never voluntarily attend, shopping trips to which we would never, left to our own devices, submit, and we enjoy these things immensely. We undertake huge tasks for love's sake—the moving of the beloved's furniture from a fifth-floor walk-up, the typing of the beloved's incomprehensible manuscript—and we count these things pleasures. We talk on the telephone together for hours; when we hang up, we ring right back: "There was something I forgot to tell you…"

Zion, in this hymn, is pictured as a young woman whose lover is approaching. The people have longed for deliverance with the fervor that we all remember from our own experience of being in love, with the same totality, the same utter focus. And now it is here.

One thing that happens when people are in love, though, is that they idealize the beloved at first. Everything is perfect. It is this euphoria that makes us love to do things we don't really enjoy, simply because the one we love enjoys them. It renders idiosyncracies charming, the same ones that will soon enough become merely annoying. Later, we wish for that old feeling, that sweeping delight that makes everything bright because we are in love.

Sometimes people then separate. "We just don't have the same magic we used to have, you know?" they sadly say as they pack their things and turn their attention toward finding another magic person.

None of us retains our magical perfection forever. For a time, it makes us godlike in each other's eyes. But we are not godlike. We are unsuitable objects for worship. Only God can sustain it. Love changes when human beings are the ones doing the loving. Only God's love is constant. When human love grows and deepens, it mirrors this constancy. So love does not make us godlike. But love can make us more godly.

Saturday in Advent I

O let us not, for evil past, be driven from thy face at last,
But with thy saints for evermore behold thee, love thee, and adore.

LATIN, CA. 7TH CENTURY; TRANS. *HYMNAL 1982*, HYMN 63

Did I do something to deserve this? People in hospitals sometimes have time on their hands, and they also often have a frightening situation that sometimes puts them in mind of their sins. However much they may know intellectually that it is not so, there is a part of them that wonders if their current state of ill health is not somehow related to some past misdeed. *Am I being punished?* And it's not just young, healthy people, laid low in their prime by some freak accident, who wonder about this; I've heard people well into their eighties wonder aloud what they have done to deserve a medical condition that any doctor would affirm to be just about what one might expect in old age.

It is common for human beings to separate from one another when one has offended; such estrangements can go on unmended for decades. "I don't want to see you anymore," one person says to another when a relationship is over. "They're not speaking," people say of another pair whose friendship has ended. It's natural that we should suppose, at first, that God is like us in this regard, shining the sun on us when we have behaved well and turning his back when we have not. We hear the people in Scripture articulating this calculus all the time: "So-and-so was king of Israel for this many years, then he did what was evil in the sight of the Lord and he died," as if old king so-and-so might have gone on forever had he not offended.

This is not how it is. God is not less present to those who have sinned. God is, in fact, more available to them, since they have a specific need to experience the divine forgiveness. They are unreconciled; whether they know it or not, they are not at peace. Their prosperity or health is not the measure of God's presence any more than it is for anyone else. The good and the bad both know misfortune in life. God is simply present to all of us, whatever our state. It was not in its virtue that humankind's readiness for Christ lay; our readiness lay, as it continues to abide, in our need.

Second Sunday of Advent

Israel's strength and consolation, hope of all the earth thou art:
Dear desire of every nation, joy of every longing heart.
<small>Charles Wesley (1707–1788), Hymn 66</small>

When the more musical of the Wesley brothers penned this hymn, the British Empire was at the peak of its power and influence. Throughout the successive colonizations that marked its expansion, the British brought their culture everywhere they went. The people they found in the places they went looked primitive to them. They needed to be civilized. Part of becoming civilized was becoming a Christian. It was assumed that everyone should be one, and would want to be one once the obvious advantages were clear. Colonization and Christianization went hand in hand.

Now, of course, we don't equate the world religions with savagery. Now there are great interfaith dialogues that are not veiled attempts to convert, but genuine explorations of how the divine love has been expressed in different places at different times. But is there any way in which it can be said without patronizing other cultures that Christ *is* the "dear desire of every nation"? What about the felicitous vision of Charles Wesley, a vision of the human family in harmony, joy in every longing heart?

Probably the best way to begin thinking about this is to leave aside the drive toward intellectual consensus in spiritual unity. We really don't all have to think alike to be in the same family. No successful family ever does: They raise their members to be most fully what God has designed each of them to be, rather than clones of each other. A Christian sees Christ at work in every human endeavor that reaches for the good, and recognizes Christ easily in other people, whether or not those people share his own precise vision of God's action in the world.

Monday in Advent II

Comfort, comfort ye my people, speak ye peace, thus saith our God;
Comfort those who sit in darkness mourning 'neath their sorrows' load.
> JOHANN G. OLEARIUS (1611–1684); TRANS. CATHERINE WINKWORTH (1827–1878),
> HYMN 67

My friend is barely able to control the shaking of her hands. "I've never been so cold in my life," she says, "I just can't get warm." And yet she is drenched with sweat. Her face is ashen, and tears stand in her eyes. After many years, she has come to understand that her use of prescription drugs has rendered her life unmanageable, and now she is in a hospital to stop. It is, far and away, the hardest thing she has ever done.

Her prayer book is next to her hospital bed. Together, we have Holy Communion: a short Scripture reading, the Lord's Prayer, then the tiny pieces of flat white bread, brought from the church in a little silver pyx. "The Body of

Christ, the bread of heaven," I say as I put a piece in her hand. We talk quietly for a bit. I touch her hand; it is not so cold. I tell her that she seems a little better.

"Peace helps," she says with a shaky smile.

"Yeah, I guess it's got to," I say. "The reverse is certainly true." I tell her again that I think she is very brave, and we part.

Life is hard, but peace helps. Many of the sorrows that beset us are things that we can do nothing about, things we simply must endure. There is no door to a drug-free life except the terrible one she's walking through, and there is no way it's going to be anything but hard. We may not have a choice about whether or not to suffer, but we can always choose how we will face suffering. Those who suffer need comfort from wherever it can be had: from God through other people and from God through the quiet voice within. In whatever form and by whatever means it comes, comfort comes from God.

Tuesday in Advent II

Make ye straight what long was crooked, make the rougher places plain;
Let your hearts be true and humble, as befits his holy reign.

JOHANN G. OLEARIUS (1611–1684); TRANS. CATHERINE WINKWORTH (1827–1878),
HYMN 67

I myself am a little crooked. After being hit by a car six years ago, my lower spine is a bit out of kilter. There is a slight lack of symmetry in my movement and even, come to think of it, in my sitting still. The only thing I can do with no pain at all is lie on my back.

It used to be much worse than it is now. I learned how to care for it with exercise and diet, so that pain is no longer the centerpiece of my days, as it was for a while. But I remember what it was like—how the search for a way out of my pain dominated me, how eagerly I bought special pillows and liniments and tried new painkillers. It was desperate, my quest for relief from pain, and it took time and energy. I found it hard to write, I recall, and—oddly—hard to pray. Everything seemed to take a lot longer than it had before the accident. The elaborate arrangements of being a person in pain left less room for being anything else. It was not only my body that was crooked; my life was crooked, too.

Straight from pain: This is how I learned that I had to work and pray. Not rising above it or working around it, functioning as if it weren't there, but straight from it. I had to allow it to tell me things about myself that I didn't want to be true: that I have limits, that I am not a superwoman, that my will is not the last word every time, that I have much more in common with the poor and weak than I used to think I had. All these things are good to know.

There is nothing we have that is really ours: no possession, no skill, no power. We can lose what we have in an instant. A serious reversal in fortune merely reveals what has always been true of us: We are dependent in all things on a power beyond ourselves. We may have trusted in our own power for years, but eventually life forces all of us to place our trust in God, who loves us no matter what befalls.

Wednesday in Advent II

What is the crying at Jordan? Who hears, O God, the prophecy?
Dark is the season, dark our hearts and shut to mystery.
<small>CAROL CHRISTOPHER DRAKE (B. 1933), HYMN 69</small>

Midnight. My snoring husband awakens me, and now the edge is off my exhaustion. I can't seem to go back to sleep. I lie there for forty minutes or so before admitting defeat. I'll get up and do some work; maybe it will be boring and I'll nod off. I creep down the stairs. The wood is cold under my bare feet, and the air is cold as well. But Q has laid a fire, I see; I decide that it is mine and light the newspaper at the base of the pile of logs. Flames engulf it gratifyingly—his fires always work, unlike mine, which only succeed about half the time.

I could watch it for hours: the lights and shadows it makes on the dark fireplace wall, the scarlet embers close to the wood, the golden licks of flame reaching unanimously up into the chimney. I am told that a fire in the fireplace is an inefficient means of acquiring heat, that I would be better off simply raising the thermostat. But that would not give me the interplay of light and darkness I crave. To be awake in the dark night, when the world is asleep, to sit in an oval of light, safe from the mute dark, to open my eyes when everyone else's eyes are closed—this is warmth of a different sort. It is free. It is out of step with the world and, in being out of step, it claims the world differently.

The prophets are always out of step. They do odd things: John the Baptist dresses oddly and eats even more oddly. Jeremiah wanders the streets of Jerusalem wearing a yoke, like the yoke a slave wears. Ezekiel sees flying saucers. The prophets are stern when everyone else is merry. They are awake when everyone else is asleep. They can be annoying people to have around. But by their self-imposed distance from normal life, they see things others miss.

Thursday in Advent II

Now comes the day of salvation, in joy and terror the Word is born!
God gives himself into our lives; O let salvation dawn!
CAROL CHRISTOPHER DRAKE (B. 1933), HYMN 69

When I was little, I always thought it odd to speak of the fear of God, that we are to love and fear God at the same time. In joy and terror? Why on earth would I love something scary?

I guess it just takes a while to grasp the fact that love *itself* is scary; appreciation isn't. You can love lots of things without fear—strawberry shortcake, your favorite song, a favorite outfit, a movie star—if you love them pallidly enough. If you love them instrumentally, as objects you can consume and enjoy and then cast aside. But real love is different: With real love comes the knowledge that it can be lost, that if I give myself to my love, I leave a piece of myself there. I can be injured. With love comes fear, the fear of losing that which I love, the fear that this love will change my life—indeed, has already done so. Appreciation leaves us more or less unchanged. Love gets us up and moving.

And often we don't want to move. We want to stay in the familiar little world we know. We will close our eyes to all manner of possibilities if we think they may disturb it. But at the end of life, what can I say about myself if I never summon the courage to love in fear? That I was very careful for years and years, and then I died?

The love of God is scary love, like all real human love. But it's not scary because we might lose it, like all our other loves, even though we are forever imagining that God is like us: punitive, whimsical, volatile. The love of God scares us precisely because that is not so, because it reveals the rest of life as extremely temporary. God's love is eternal, and no other love is like that. It is not the love of God that we will lose. It is everything else.

Friday in Advent II

He comes, the prisoners to release in Satan's bondage held;
The gates of brass before him burst, the iron fetters yield.
PHILIP DODDRIDGE (1702–1751), HYMN 71

The young woman shakes her head grimly, not looking at me. "That's not the problem," she says. I've just suggested, as I have done before, that some of the grimness of her life might be alleviated by psychotherapy. "Well, it's certainly not the *whole* problem," I respond, "but it might help with *part* of the whole problem." She shakes her head again and sighs. I decide to try again tomorrow.

She's not mistaken: Many of the things that cause her pain do arise from outside of her—a tight job market, for instance, was not caused by her depression. But the paralysis that prevents her from navigating it is. It feels to her as if all her problems are caused by other peoples' actions, or by forces beyond her control. But only some of them are. We all face a life heavily influenced by people and processes beyond our control. It is our response to those things that determines whether or not it will be a happy life. And whether or not it will be free.

The people who looked for their Messiah almost always mentioned the freeing of those in captivity as part of his redeeming work. Israel certainly knew about captivity: the memory of slavery in Egypt, exile in Babylonia, the current occupation of their country by Rome, gross examples of aggressive coercion by others. But their prophets never let them forget about the bondage they also created for themselves, the self-made prisons formed by the inevitable consequences of their own habits and actions. There was poverty in Israel because there was greed in Israel, the prophets pointed out; the two go together. We are not necessarily free just because somebody else isn't oppressing us. Then as now, corporately or singly, we are more than capable of ruining things for ourselves.

Saturday in Advent II

He comes, the broken heart to bind, the bleeding soul to cure;
And with the treasures of his grace to enrich the humble poor.

PHILIP DODDRIDGE (1702–1751), HYMN 71

The main thing I learned when I was on the waterfront was that most Americans are very fortunate. I met thousands of people for whom rights we take for granted represent unimaginable privilege: people who are not allowed a day off for weeks at a time, people who are not allowed to go ashore after having been at sea for weeks or months, people who are not allowed to seek medical treatment. The most common inequity, though, one so common that it was virtually unnoticed, was the complete absence on most vessels of the concept of equal pay for equal work. A Greek and a Filipino could work side by side painting the very same surface, and the Greek would earn five times what the Filipino was given. And nobody complained. Or a German and a Sri Lankan. Poor nations export seafarers like we export scrap metal, and their poverty is a powerful selling point: Their situation at home is so desperate that they'll work for anything and be right glad of it.

The well-to-do sometimes have a certain mythology with regard to the poor that centers on the conviction that they don't have the same needs as other people. It goes still further—that there is a rightness, a goodness to their poverty, that it somehow confers a spiritual integrity on them that the rich don't have. We see poor people from another culture sing together, or dance, or play, and we tell ourselves that they, not we, have the secret of true happiness. We tell each other, pensively, that money can't buy happiness. It almost seems to us that it would be a shame to spoil the simple joys of the poor by making them rich.

In his great classic, *A Christmas Carol*, Charles Dickens begins to seduce us with this sentimental idea of the poor. The Cratchitts are so much happier than wretched, miserly Scrooge! But Dickens doesn't let us off the hook with this self-serving thought. Tiny Tim may die of his poverty, we come to see, and the thing that will prevent that tragedy is the generosity of the rich, not their romanticization of his neediness. There is nothing ennobling about being poor. It drains the soul. Generosity of spirit is harder, not easier. Like it or not, the moral economy of God is not predicated on the necessity of poverty for most and riches for some.

Third Sunday of Advent

Shine forth, and let they light restore
Earth's own true loveliness once more.

CHARLES COFFIN (1676–1749); TRANS. CHARLES WINFRED DOUGLAS (1867–1944), AFTER JOHN CHANDLER (1806–1876), HYMN 76

One of the oldest notions about Jesus is the idea that he is the second Adam. God made a perfect world, into which sin and death were introduced by the devil. Things went from bad to worse for a long time after that, and then Christ came to undo the damage Adam had done. For, as in Adam all die, St. Paul explains around the year 55 or 60 A.D., so also in Christ shall all be made alive (1 Cor. 15:22). Thus, medieval art depicting the crucifixion often shows the bones of Adam buried in the earth under the cross.

People recovering from an addiction to alcohol or drugs understand this mythic idea from personal experience. They know all too well what it is to put something else in the place of God in their lives, to sacrifice everything—family, career, health, friendship—on the deadly altar of their habit. "You will not die," coos the serpent to a credulous Eve (Gen. 3:4), and any alcoholic recognizes the voice.

Many also recognize the voice of the new Adam: that loving Higher Power that alone can restore them to sanity. Of course, the voice of the new Adam sounds from the cross. It is honest, promising salvation but not a carefree walk through life. "I hated the sober life," a man who had slipped back into his out-of-control drinking habit told me. I can understand that. Sober, he had to face painful realities against which he had been accustomed to anesthetizing himself.

Life *can* be hard. How can we live through it? We survive what life dishes out by doing in our lives what alcoholics learn to do in their meetings: be honest about ourselves, reach out for help when we need it, band together with sisters and brothers to help one another, learn to slow down and be mindful of the only behavior we can really control—our own. The paradox is that those who have in this way rescued their lives from chaos come to understand that they really haven't rescued themselves at all—that all of the things that kept them whole and serene are part of a larger love in which their own wills rest safely. What is true for those who have been raised from the living death of addiction is true for all of us: *All* of our strength comes from God.

Monday in Advent III

O come, O come, Emmanuel, and ransom captive Israel,
That mourns in lonely exile here until the Son of God appear.

LATIN, CA. 9TH CENTURY; VER. *HYMNAL 1940*, HYMN 56

My brother died recently. I notice, since it happened, that I have not been as efficient as I usually am. That I seem to have little energy these days, and little concentration. I seem to want to sleep too much. People tell me I look tired; I glance at the mirror, and it is so.

Mourning is really all about loneliness. We are a little more alone when someone we care about has died, a little closer to the final loneliness of our own end. As a Christian, I rejoice in David's entry into a larger life. But my feelings lag far behind; as a sister, I have lost a piece of myself. "Are your parents living?" somebody asks. I say that they are not and suddenly feel young and small.

Interesting. I am far from alone. I have another brother. I have a husband and children. I have good friends and a satisfying career. My world is full of good things. So, I imagine, were the worlds of many people in the Israel that "mourned in lonely exile." Families, food, work, shelter, a rich heritage of faith, and a common memory binding everyone together in comforting familiarity—they had these things. But they longed for a Messiah anyway.

We are not satisfied. We live in longing. St. Augustine said so: "Our souls find no rest until they rest in thee," he wrote in his *Confessions*, a book addressed in the second person to God. Times of specific loss may remind us of that, but it is really true all the time. Surrounded by people, we are yet so separate.

"He's in a better place," people told me at the funeral, and indeed he is. An existence in which nothing is lost, all is restored, all estrangement overcome. Where all of us—the living, who don't experience it yet, and the dead who do—are in Christ, and Christ is all in all.

Tuesday in Advent III

Your cradle shines with glory's light; Its splendor pierces all our gloom.
ATTRIB. AMBROSE OF MILAN (340–397); TRANS. CHARLES P. PRICE (B. 1920), HYMN 55

You pick yours out of a phalanx of twenty identical pink-and-blue-plaid blankets in the hospital. Almost immediately you recognize the cry that belongs to your baby, and your soundest sleep is broken immediately when you hear that cry at night. For the rest of your days, you are something other than a free agent. Once upon a time, such an arrangement would have seemed like bondage to you. Now it feels perfectly normal. You come to consider a night during which you awaken only once or twice to be a good night's sleep.

The balance between God-given freedom and an equally God-given responsibility is not always easy to maintain when there is a baby in the picture. You are who you were before, but your freedom is different. Looking back, it appears that it was absolute in those days. You can barely remember what it was like.

But nobody's personal freedom is absolute. Parents are not the only people who bear responsibility to others. We all have duties; none of us is an island. Those who try to live for themselves alone find that happiness eludes them again and again. It is not our way: our way is to live in community.

The complete vulnerability of the Christ child involves us in this community. Christ comes to save humanity, but he comes in the form of one who is in need of human care. The splendor in which Jesus is born is not the lonely splendor of autonomy but the warmer splendor of love, love that makes us better than we were.

Wednesday in Advent III

O come, thou Branch of Jesse's tree, free them from Satan's tyranny
That trust thy mighty power to save, and give them victory o'er the grave.
<small>LATIN, CA. 9TH CENTURY; VER. *HYMNAL 1940*, HYMN 56</small>

The Last Judgment was a favorite scene in medieval art. The presentation of it was standard: The righteous stand together in choirlike groups, either at the right hand of Jesus, who sits in the center, or surrounding him on both sides. The unrighteous are on the left, or somewhere near the bottom of the painting, in the darkness of hell. The righteous all look pretty much alike: lovely white robes, composed expressions. To tell the truth, they are boring in their homogeneity. The really interesting people in these paintings are the damned. These anonymous artists understood their mission to be a moral one, to scare the dickens out of the folks who would behold these paintings out of the corners of their eyes every Sunday. Just how sinners would be punished was depicted in detail. We see them being disemboweled, roasted alive, skewered on pitchforks, torn limb from limb, raped in various horrific ways, eaten with relish by fantastic hungry animals—there was no end to the gruesomeness of the medieval imagination where the torments of the damned were concerned. Some attempt was often made to suit the punishment to the crime; the avaricious, for instance, might be shown being force-fed golden coins, or the jealous simmering away on the coals of their own obsession, or the sexual sinner raped in some particularly wretched way.

The vindictiveness of the whole project is off-putting to us now: We are much more apt to think of punishment in terms of eventual rehabilitation than of vengeance. Theirs was a different age. But it survives in us. Every execution currently carried out in the United States is accompanied by two sets of sounds: the sound of prayer from those who gather outside the prison walls to bear witness against state-sanctioned killing and the sound of cheers from an enthusiastic crowd nearby—ordinary people who load the kids into the station wagon with a nice picnic and make an evening of it, a death-penalty tailgate party.

But God does not rejoice in human suffering or desire the death of a sinner. God desires that we may turn from evil and do good. Christ's presence within each human heart makes it possible. Christ's presence in human history makes bringing it about a human duty.

Thursday in Advent III

O come, Desire of nations, bind in one the hearts of all mankind;
Bid thou our sad divisions cease, and be thyself our King of Peace.

LATIN, CA. 9TH CENTURY; VER. *HYMNAL 1940*, HYMN 56

A recent and very popular movie entertained audiences with the fantasy that the President of the United States might deliberately involve us in a war in order to boost his approval ratings in an election year. It is a fact that our economy has often been helped by going to war: An army marches on its stomach and the mobilization effort requires goods and services, from nuclear submarines to body bags. But the chilling idea that those entrusted with the common good might choose warfare in order to advance their own interests was fascinating to many of us: It sold a lot of tickets.

For some of us, our "sad divisions" are *not* sad at all; they're exciting and sometimes downright fun. We sing songs about them: our national anthem is about a bomb attack. They energize us, fill us with common purpose and patriotism, and produce in some of us remarkable heroism—all in the service of vanquishing the foe. But whatever virtues may be brought to bear in time of war, however stirring a thing war may seem, it is nonetheless all about the taking of human life and, therefore, tragic. The unity it produces is a fraud: It is a unity that can flourish only in the arid soil of a much larger disunity. It must be fed and watered with hatred.

The divisions of humankind spawn new divisions, more and more of them all the time. People can usually find it in their hearts to do again what they once have done. War, so unthinkable at first, quickly comes to seem reasonable. A man who had killed at least a hundred people in battle told a friend that very early in that count they all began to look alike. He knew that they were aiming for his heart, as he aimed for theirs, and that was about all there was to it.

God cherishes each one of us as a beloved child throughout the whole of life and beyond. I've not been to heaven, but I suspect that its music is not a martial tune. The dead do not all look alike to the God in whose image we all are created.

Friday in Advent III

O come, O come, thou Lord of might, who to thy tribes on Sinai's height,
In ancient times didst give the law, in cloud, and majesty, and awe.

LATIN, CA. 9TH CENTURY; VER. *HYMNAL 1940*, HYMN 56

I go to court with people sometimes. I go to housing court, which in New York is something of a cross between a cattle auction and a gangster funeral. I go to criminal court with poor people sometimes, at which the defendants meet their bored lawyers for the first time out in the hallway, minutes before the trial begins. I testify in civil suites sometimes—a tad more elegant, usually, and not as noisy.

Believe it or not, there is a majesty in any courtroom. Not even the self-serving dealing of traffic court, not even the braying confusion of housing court, not even the cynicism of criminal court can completely erase the dignity of the human decision to live under the rule of law. That some choose not to do so does not injure this dignity. We stand when the judge enters the courtroom, stand in deference to what we have invested in her, in respect for the sanity she represents in the midst of the chaos soon to be presented in evidence.

"Cloud, and majesty, and awe." God appeared to Moses in a burning bush. The divine might was revealed to the Israelites in the series of miracles that preceded their release from bondage in Egypt, culminating in their stunning deliverance at the Red Sea. All manner of odd and wondrous things happened to the people during their sojourn in the desert: Water gushed from barren rock, manna "magically" appeared on the ground when they were starving. There was no shortage of special effects. But the lasting product of all these miraculous signs was not more miracles. It was, instead, a way of life. What endured in the common life was the one thing that could sustain a community—not miracles and wonders, but the law. This people would be defined not primarily by power but by righteousness. And we who are their heirs mirror the divine righteousness in our law, no matter how secular it is or we are, no matter how far below the divine perfection we may have fallen. "All rise!" says the bailiff, and we struggle to our feet, nowhere near as good as we ought to be but able, nonetheless, to acknowledge our need for a measure of the good.

Saturday in Advent III

O come, thou Wisdom from on high, who orderest all things mightily;
To us the path of knowledge show, and teach us in her ways to go.

LATIN, CA. 9TH CENTURY; VER. *HYMNAL 1940*, HYMN 56

I would learn to read in the first grade, I was told as a young child, and I couldn't wait to go. As it was, I was dependent on the schedules of the adults around me for stories, having to wait until there was somebody who could read to me. I feasted on pictures in the fairy-tale books, of course, and made up stories with my dolls. And we had a television, which had more stories. And there were stories on the radio as well. But my parents and my brothers read happily in silence for hours. Sometimes you would have to call the boys' names twice, or even three times, before you could get them to look up from their books. Reading was that absorbing. I longed to join the club.

Somehow I had the impression that I would learn to read that first day, that learning to read was just a secret that would be imparted to me at the proper time, that I would learn to read in much the same way that I would learn where to hang my coat and where the lunchroom was. I didn't grasp that learning to read was a process. Imagine my frustration, then, when we began to go over the alphabet and the sounds each letter signified. That was all very well. "But when are we going to learn to read?" I asked the teacher as the afternoon wore on. She told me this *was* learning to read, that this was how you started. Oh. This was the biggest disappointment my short life had yet encountered. I trudged home and found my grandmother, who read me a story. For old times' sake.

Soon, the thrill of the chase took over. It *was* fun to sound out the words on the page, to begin to recognize a whole word, to read and write longer and longer sentences. But it was work, too. To grow in wisdom doesn't just happen to us, while we sit there with our hands folded in our laps and do nothing. We acquire wisdom. We pursue wisdom. We follow in her ways.

Dear Reader,

Now look, things can get a little tricky here on out from year to year.

Sometimes the Fourth Sunday of Advent falls on Christmas Eve. It happened a few years ago, and it made for some pretty heavy church that Sunday, let me tell you.

In any case, some day in the course of this coming week will be Christmas Eve, so you'll need to turn a few pages to get back on track. The days following Christmas are just dated, since there's no way of knowing year to year what day of the week they will fall on.

There are some things in life we just have to accept.

Fourth Sunday of Advent

Those dear tokens of his passion still his dazzling body bears,
Cause of endless exultation to his ransomed worshipers...
With what rapture gaze we on those glorious scars!
CHARLES WESLEY (1707–1788), HYMN 58

Recently, some ancient statues found in Eastern Europe and in Turkey have suggested that a very different culture prevailed there tens of thousands of years ago. The statues are female, round and fecund with large breasts—symbols of fertility. The culture that produced them, say those who have worked on them, was a culture that celebrated life, that found the primary mystery of life in birth and reproduction. Its central religious figures were women. It was communal. It was not warlike.

With a certain sadness, those who study this ancient society speak of its defeat by another group, one that survived by conquest and organized its ethics and its value system according to categories necessary for fighting. Hierarchy became important, along with strength and private property. And, in its religion, the central mystery was no longer birth; it was death.

They could be describing us, actually. That's how we look to people who don't understand us. We wear the first-century equivalent of electric chairs around our necks. Our central devotional object is usually the figure of a dying man, or a dead one. His wounds still bleed. We talk of eating his body and drinking his blood. Step back for a moment and imagine what all this would look like to someone who had never seen it.

Well, okay. It's certainly true that Christianity has abetted its share of war and conquest. But the mystery of birth and the love of life are far from absent in it. We don't choose death. It happens to us whether we like it or not. But we do enter death in order to reach life, affirming that what we see here is not all there is. We affirm life as a gift from a God who causes life, the world as God's beloved creation. Unlike the devotees of the voluptuous goddesses, though, we don't worship life itself. It is beautiful, but it can also be very sad. And it is passing away.

Monday in Advent IV

Lo! the Lamb, so long expected, comes with pardon down from heaven;
Let us haste, with tears of sorrow, one and all to be forgiven;
So when next he comes with glory, and the world is wrapped in fear,
May he with his mercy shield us, and with words of love draw near.

LATIN, CA. 6TH CENTURY; TRANS. *HYMNS ANCIENT AND MODERN*, 1861, HYMN 59

I have known the young man since he was a teenager; now, he is in his thirties. His mother, who died just last week, was a close friend. She was a private person, formal and dignified in her manner. She died as she had lived: quietly, without any fuss, checking herself into the hospital Thursday evening and gone Friday afternoon. He found a note on his apartment door; "Call the hospital," it said. His shock and sorrow are compounded with guilt. Why hadn't he known? Why hadn't she called? Why hadn't he called *her* that last night? He was a fine son to her, and she was proud of him. Telling him that right now, though, does little good. Right now he is alone with his self-recriminations. He'll get the big picture, a picture that includes some self-pardon, in a little while.

Once a person has a few decades under his or her belt, it is certain that there will be a few parts of the record that occasion heartfelt regret. I can think of a number of things that I wish with all my heart I had not done. Some of them, like the missed good-bye that fills this young man with guilt right now, are not sins. Some of them are, but they had an extenuating circumstance or two that make them a bit easier to swallow. But some didn't. They were just sinful, and I regret them. Whatever I told myself or anyone else at the time, they were wrong.

In some cases, you can make amends directly to someone you have injured. In others, you can't. Rarely can you undo the bad effects of such a thing; what's done usually stays done. What's really needed is not an explanation or an excuse or even restitution. What's needed is pardon. And it really doesn't matter whether or not anyone else thinks it's a sin. You're the one who has to live with it. The need for pardon is yours alone. And after that, pardon is between you and God.

Tuesday in Advent IV

In sorrow that the ancient curse should doom to death a universe,
You came, O Savior, to set free
Your own in glorious liberty.

LATIN, 9TH CENTURY; VER. *HYMNAL 1940*, HYMN 60

My friend is an artist—crochet is her medium. She is so far above my pink, white, and blue chain-stitched baby-blanket level that I can look at her work only with mute admiration. Afghans, sweaters, handbags, entire coats—she is a Michelangelo of yarn. She wasn't always Michelangelo, though.

Michelangelo used to tell people that when he approached a block of marble, he knew that it had within it the statue that would eventually emerge. His task was to chip away the stone from around that shape within it so that it could be seen. The stone itself told him what to do.

My friend didn't do that—not at first. She wanted to plan each project perfectly and have it turn out just as she expected. And it did, of course; it was perfect.

But for a long time, although she honed the technical skill of her craft to what certainly looked to me like perfection, she was not free. It wasn't quite art. Not until she learned to allow the yarn to instruct *her*, to show her how hue and texture might combine and vary, did poetry begin to emerge under her hands.

We talked from time to time as she explored this. About how her art mirrored her life, about learning to sit still and listen to what life might be telling her, rather than trying to manage it into someone else's perfection. About how free art is, and how free life can be, and how trustworthy.

"Here, I have something for you," she said one day, as she withdrew a small object from her purse. It was a rock, covered with crocheted yarn in different weights and different shades of blue, worked all around the outside of it with different stitches until the rock was completely covered. "Terrific," I said. "It kind of goes with the room," and it does. But it also goes with the talks about God's action in her life that we have had in this room. It is a sculpture of unexpectedness, of not knowing exactly where you will be led when you set out. A sculpture of a journey into trust.

Wednesday in Advent IV

Still he comes within us, still his voice would win us
From the sins that hurt us, would to Truth convert us.

JAN ROH (1485?–1547); TRANS. CATHERINE WINKWORTH (1827–1878), HYMN 53

A few weeks before Christmas, I think it was. It was snowing, great fat flakes swirling in front of the windshield as we drove into town. We were going to one of the four nice clothing stores in our town to buy my mother a winter coat. I remember everything: the warm wooden floors, the three-way mirror before which my mother stood, appraising the two coats that had made the final cut. My father, in his overcoat standing nearby, his felt hat in his hands.

One of the coats was green, and I didn't like it. The other was a gorgeous mid-calf sweep of soft black wool. "Which one do you like, Barbara?" my mother asked me, and suddenly I was afraid. What if I chose the wrong one? What if I chose the one she liked less, saddling my own mother for years to come with a coat she didn't want to wear? By now, I had fallen in love with the black coat and thoroughly loathed the green one. But what if the coat I liked cost too much money, and in choosing it I inflicted a mortal wound on the family exchequer? Suddenly, I seemed possessed of much too much power.

"Which one costs less?" I asked loudly. The saleslady heard me and frowned; my mother looked embarrassed and my father looked annoyed. A question I had thought would seem responsible and grown-up appeared to have backfired; it turned out to be a nuisance. I had been given a chance to express my preference and I had blown it. When would I ever learn?

I vividly remember every one of my juvenile humiliations, self-inflicted or otherwise. Almost all of them had sprung from my uninformed desire to do the right thing before I really knew what the right thing was. Kids deduce most of what they know, and they rarely score a bulls-eye their first time out. They usually need some help in forming an accurate picture of the world.

But actually, nobody gets it right all the time. God must have known when Adam and Eve had that first nibble of forbidden fruit that eventually he would have to come himself and make things right. Patiently, through the millennia of human history, God has shown us the truth. Why else but because he knows that we won't get it without some help?

Thursday in Advent IV

Lord, give us grace to awake us,
To see the branch that begins to bloom;
In great humility is hid
All heaven in a little room.

CAROL CHRISTOPHER DRAKE (B. 1933), HYMN 69

I should have gotten the Christmas tree earlier in the season. I had a Norman Rockwell fantasy about Q and me taking the grandchildren to pick it out, but I forgot that the semester ends just before Christmas, so he's up to his eyeballs in blue books right now. I can delay no longer.

There aren't too many trees left in the lot. One of the remaining ones is nice, though: big and fat, a little twisted at the bottom, which is probably why it's still there, but the man in charge assures me he can trim it and make it right. This turns out to be considerably easier said than done; he calls in a colleague and they struggle with it for half an hour, as I begin to despair quietly of its having any trunk left at all when they're done. Eventually, I persuade the two of them to give up, and I drag the thing home to Q. He prevails, naturally, and soon I am hanging all our old ornaments on the branches. They hail from all our walks of life—from the grandchildren's babyhood and our children's childhood, from my own childhood and his—ornaments made in nursery schools by little hands long ago, yearly witnesses of family joy and sorrow, of brokenness, and love in the midst of brokenness, silent markers of the passing of time.

"This winter hasn't been anything to write home about," I remark as I trim the tree and he grades exams. A few flurries, one or two days of below-freezing temperatures. "It's not normal," people keep saying to one another uneasily, trying to remember exactly what El Niño is again, and what it does, waiting for the other shoe to drop. "February's going to be really something this year. I can feel it in my bones."

Well, maybe it will and maybe it won't. But even if we're not up to our necks in snow this winter, it's certainly not spring. The leaves are gone and the ground is no longer green. All nature is quiet. Quiet and dead-looking.

But it is not really dead. Life waits just beneath the cold surface of the ground. The buds of next year's flowers swell the forsythia branches out front; if we bring a few inside in a few weeks, they will warm up and burst into brilliant yellow bloom. When we're finished with the Christmas tree, Q will cut its branches off and cover other plants' roots with them: a blanket to keep them soft and warm. Now, laden with the cheery, battered emblems of dozens of bitter-sweet Christmas memories, the tree warms our hearts in that peculiar way that only a Christmas tree can. And later, its branches will do other things, until at last they return to the earth. To do it all again.

Friday in Advent IV

Not, as of old, a little child,
To bear, and fight, and die...

GREEK; TRANS. JOHN BROWNLIE (1859–1925), HYMN 73

The children in the after-school program have their Christmas pageant today, the last day before they leave for the holiday. For several weeks now, we have stolen what time we could from the time allotted for homework to rehearse. I have picked out clumsy Christmas carols on the ridiculous electric keyboard, which is our only instrument, and they have gone over and over the story.

The children who represent the city of Bethlehem have paraded repeatedly out from the wings in a line, wearing cardboard boxes painted to look like Middle Eastern houses with cutout windows. Joseph enters from stage right, pulling Mary in a wagon. The shepherds have made their entrance over and over again from stage left, leading the sheep, who crawl in on all fours, wearing men's white tee shirts on their heads, the sleeves knotted to hang down like sheep's ears. One of the sheep is much taller than the other children; much thought was given to the proper role for Sean, who is autistic, before we realized that he would be a perfect sheep, with a shepherd to guide him. The angels greet them and everyone kneels before the baby. The three Wise Men have had a hard time waiting for their individual cues; I keep seeing more Wise Men at one time than "We Three Kings" entitles me to see thus far. I am having a difficult time communicating to them the importance of the progression inherent in their roles. The two narrators argue passionately about who will wear a certain luridly sequined dress; I wish I had never grabbed it from the parish thrift shop in my costuming frenzy earlier this week. One of them declares, as the house lights dim, that she will not participate. I hiss that it is too late for that now, and the show begins.

The parents, exhausted from their work week and their Christmas preparations, sit in rows and peer around each other for a glimpse of that particular little face, the face of the child for whom they struggle through every difficult day. I have misplaced my glasses and can barely read the music for the Christmas carols; each wrong note from the wretched keyboard sounds very loud to me, but nobody seems to mind. The occupants of the houses of Bethlehem peek at the actions through their windows; Zachary keeps popping out of his to see if it's over yet. And, finally, it is.

Life is hard for these children and their parents. They are the working poor, for the most part. Many of the families are headed by a single parent: women mostly, mothers and grandmothers, but a few men. Not much money, not much room, not much leisure. Our lumpy pageant rings true, here. It was to just such a family that the Christ child came. A wave of love rolls toward the performers as the audience applauds vigorously. "That was wonderful," everyone says as we shake hands and wish one another a Merry Christmas. And so it was.

The Eve of Christ's Nativity

By those who truly listen his voice is truly heard.

You just believe in all this stuff because you want it to be true! People who don't believe sometimes say that with an air of triumph, as if they'd just discovered the fatal flaw that will bring down the whole religious enterprise. As if the element of volition in faith were news.

But *of course* we want it to be true. That's why we're here. If we didn't want it to be true, we'd believe in something else. Faith is not compelled by facts or evidence. It is a matter of the spirit, not just the mind—although the mind is a useful thing, and it would certainly be hard to think about faith without it. We see the same things everyone else sees: the same wonders, the same miseries. We don't live in a reality different from other people's. We're all in the same boat.

Hardly anybody who was alive at the time Jesus was born believed him to be the Messiah. Just a few shepherds and three old men from out of town. Many people would see and hear him, but not believe—so many that, in a few years, it would be possible for his enemies to kill him without raising much of a ruckus at all. Modern people are not the only ones who have a hard time believing. And evidence doesn't seem to have much to do with it one way or the other.

Yet, some of us hear Christ and some of us don't. Something has happened that has made us want to order our lives according to his presence and not his absence. We see that the hand of God is the good that can come out of great evil, acknowledging all the while that this good does not make evil any less evil than it was before. We desire the presence of Jesus, and so we begin to see it everywhere. Christ is born in us, and so we are reborn into our own lives. The cross stands beside our own suffering, and so we claim the empty tomb as well.

The Nativity of Our Lord Jesus Christ

The hopes and fears of all the years are met in thee tonight.
PHILLIPS BROOKS (1835–1893), HYMN 78

We finally made it home from church at 2:00 A.M. There were still a few presents left to wrap, so I made the same weary calculation I make every Christmas morning at 2:00 A.M.: What among these things can just go to their recipients *au naturel?* It doesn't take me as long as it used to to conclude that they all can, and we stumble upstairs. There is, after all, Lessons and Carols at ten this morning, and that is just a few hours away. And the opening of the gifts after that. And Christmas dinner to be made after that.

To make this time of year a time when the hopes and fears of those in my care are somehow touched and engaged is a challenge. It's not good enough just to get everything done and have it look perfect. In fact, it's not even really important to do that. What is really important is that the people who experience

Christmas through me see Christ. And so it really doesn't matter if a gift is wrapped. What matters is that its recipient feels the love it embodies.

I think I'll make the dinner a buffet instead of a sit-down meal. Less Dickensian, to be sure, but also a lot less work, and the girls can play with their new toys while we eat. I can get it on the table and then just flop in a chair. Our living room during a dinner such as that is like a Brueghel painting: lots of people together doing lots of different things, interacting and not interacting by turns. It feels safe like a Brueghel painting, too, stable. "This is our little world," the people in the painting say. "We belong here."

The world of Brueghel is long gone, of course. Its apparent stability did not protect it. The industrious, jolly people in it are all dead, and have been for centuries. Their lives were really not all that jolly even: They were stalked and felled by disease and war. Their average life expectancy was somewhere in the forties. There was abundant fear, as there is for us. We'll all be gone someday, too. This living room full of someone else's grandchildren, this house torn down, this whole town, someday, just a memory. And then, eventually, no longer even memory. The fire crackles reassuringly in the fireplace, and we feel safe. But we are passing away. All the years of all the peoples' hopes and fears meet in the Christ who was before them all and will be after they all have passed away. Our hope is not in our own safety, however industriously we may provide for it. Our hope is in something larger than our own lives—larger, even, than the life of this world we love so much.

December 26 Feast of St. Stephen

Willingly this yoke I take,
And this sacrifice I make,
Heaping joys for thee.

JEAN MAUBURN (1460–1503); TRANS. ELIZABETH RUNDLE CHARLES (1828–1896),
HYMN 97

Martyrdom has gotten a bad rap in recent years. "Oh, never mind, if you're going to be a martyr about it," we're apt to say when we think somebody we love begrudges us a favor for which we have asked them. We think that a martyr's purpose is to make us feel guilty.

But guilt has nothing to do with martyrdom. Real martyrs have nothing to do with making other people feel guilty, or with grudging self-sacrifice for which a later payment will be required. Real martyrs are about love and joy—love deep enough to sacrifice the gift of life itself, joy in life deep enough to make the leaving of it painful. Martyrs don't hate their lives—Where would be the sacrifice in surrendering something that yielded no delight? Martyrs love their lives. But they know that there are those things in the world that outweigh them in importance. Martyrs grasp the big picture.

Not many of us do. Martyrdom has always been a minority gift. It has never been given to many, so nobody ever has to feel guilty for not being one. But we can hear their stories and be inspired to widen our own gaze, to see more of the big picture ourselves. Maybe I can be braver than I think I can when trouble comes my way, as it certainly will now and then.

Love makes us more than we are, and martyrdom has everything to do with love. Part of what love is involves the welfare of another as equal in value to one's own welfare. Love makes us bigger and braver than we were, and better. And it makes us happier. St. Stephen said he saw the glory of God at the moment in which he died for the faith that had transformed his life.

Is the day after Christmas an odd day to celebrate martyrdom? Not if you separate it from guilt that has nothing whatever to do with it. Martyrdom is all about love. The coming of Christ is all about love, too.

December 27   Feast of St. John

Of the Father's love begotten, ere the worlds began to be,
He is Alpha and Omega, he the source, the ending he.

MARCUS AURELIUS CLEMENS PRUDENTIUS (348–410?); TRANS. JOHN MASON NEALE (1818–1866) AND HENRY WILLIAMS BAKER (1821–1877), HYMN 82

Now nobody could accuse St. John of not having gotten the big picture. Jesus is so different in his Gospel from the Jesus shown to us by Matthew, Mark, and Luke: no baby, no shepherds, no Wise Men, no angels, no nothing. The Christmas card business would be a very different industry if John's Gospel were the only one we had. "In the beginning was the Word, and the Word was with God, and the Word was God," he begins, and we barely know what that means.

We like the pictures better, of course. They are snapshots from our own lives, after all: our mangers, our cattle, our sheep, our babies, our moms and dads. Our fantasy wizards and kings. Angels who look like us, except with wings and halos. The birth narratives we love and know by heart connect Christ with a human history, but they are not confined to it. This history is infinitely more mysterious. It is not just us. It is more.

Other gods and their religions have come to earth, of course. The Greek gods did it all the time. Zeus liked to come in the form of an animal or a man so he could date mortal women. The gods would take sides in human conflict, playing human beings like chess pieces. Those gods were larger and mightier versions of ourselves, with larger and mightier versions of our own piques and prejudices. They had no particular love for humankind, being primarily occupied with their own affairs.

St. John's austere beginning to his austere Gospel shows us the gulf between the homely comings and goings of human history and the awesome power that brought all things into being. Sure, it's hard to understand the Incarnation. In fact, if we're hoping to understand it in this life, we'll be disappointed. Because it is so devoid of storytelling warmth, it may be hard to feel God's love in it. But John's Gospel, which begins so abstractly, is also the Gospel in which we are told that Jesus wept over the death of his friend Lazarus. The only Gospel in which we see Jesus cry. So there is human love and divine love: one love, of love begotten.

December 28   The Holy Innocents

O Rachel, cease your weeping; they're free from pain and cares.
Lord, grant us crowns as brilliant and lives as pure as theirs.

HORATIO BOLTON NELSON (1823–1913); VER. *HYMNAL 1982*, HYMN 231

I wonder if Horatio Bolton Nelson ever lost a child. It's quite likely that he did, given the time period in which he lived. So many families in those days knew that unnatural grief. I suppose he must have thought this advice would be comforting to others. Maybe he found it so himself.

Most bereaved parents I know would find it offensive—Oh, don't be sad, life is hard and your little one is better off for not having to live it. Most of us would give our lives in a heartbeat if it would give life to the children we have lost. Life is hard, but human beings are hard-wired to love it. We want to live it fully. And, more than we want to live it ourselves, we want our children to live it.

A woman comes to see me. She has lost two adult children and her husband. She plans to attend a concert of a musical group her son used to love. "Do you think maybe I shouldn't go?" she asks anxiously. "My friend tells me I should get on with my life." I tell her that I think she *is* getting on with her life; she's taking care of business, she's raising an orphaned grandchild. Let her go to the concert and feel a happy memory for a few hours. Honoring the memory of the beloved dead isn't wallowing. Studiously avoiding any mention of them is what's unnatural. It delays healing. And it's not the truth.

Her husband is also dead—the one person in the world who loved the children in the same way she did. The one person in the world who had shared their whole lives. "It's really funny," she said, "but half the time I miss him more." She stopped and corrected herself: "No, not more. I mean, I miss him taking care of me when I miss them. He took such good care of me." She smiles at a memory. "I guess I was spoiled."

Spoiled? Odd word. It suggests that we are somehow ruined by being lovingly treated. But it is her little smile that tells me that she is anything but spoiled by having been loved, that she is healing. Love doesn't spoil us, even if we are sad when we lose its daily physical presence. Love doesn't spoil us. Love makes us stronger, makes us know our worth, makes us know what joy is, even if it is now seen only through the lens of sorrow.

What's true is that nothing can take from us the fact that they have lived and that we have loved them. Nothing can change the fact that their lives were tremendous gifts in our lives, that the love we had for them was the best love we know about, that it made us much of what we are.

December 29

Child, for us sinners poor and in the manger,
We would embrace thee, with love and awe;
Who would not love thee, loving us so dearly?...
O come, let us adore him, Christ, the Lord.

JOHN FRANCIS WADE (1711–1786); TRANS. FREDERICK OAKELEY (1802–1880)
AND OTHERS, HYMN 83

There was a time when little girls wanted to be brides when they grew up, as if being a bride were a kind of job, like being a nurse or a teacher. I did when I was little, and I had a bride dress, which I wore and wore until it fell apart. As I recall, it was primarily the clothes that attracted me to the vocation. I don't remember ever fantasizing about a groom, or even being aware that brides were people who were entering a relationship.

Young adulthood is different, though. More informed and, therefore, more anxious. People begin to wonder about a life partner: Will anyone ever love me?

How will I know if it's right? And people who aren't so young have their anxieties. There are lots of single-again people of a certain age: people who haven't dated in forty years, people half-ashamed of being lonely but not too old to long for love to come again. Will I always be alone? Will I ever love again? Will anyone ever love me?

The most attractive thing in any person is lovingness. It's pretty hard not to love someone who genuinely loves us. There are those who romantically fall in love with someone with whom a romantic love is not possible; when that love is genuine, it is able to transpose itself into another kind of love, something more brotherly or sisterly, but no less dear. But, whatever kind of love is possible, the fact remains that genuine love never misses its mark. Love evokes love.

The love of God is like that. We rise to it when we learn to see it in every breath we are given, every joy, and every beauty—when we awaken to the magnitude of the gift of everything in life.

December 30

Beneath the heavenly hymn have rolled two thousand years of wrong;
And warring humankind hears not the tidings which they bring;
O hush the noise and cease your strife and hear the angels sing.

EDMUND H. SEARS (1810–1876), HYMN 89

Angels, of course, aren't our departed relatives newly fitted out with wings and a glamorous address. Angels are beings created to serve God in heaven. Some of them are charged with bringing specific messages to this or that human being. They are the communications department of heaven—God's messengers.

Are they real? I suppose that depends on what we mean by "real." Most religious propositions are best evaluated with reference to their meaning, not to their conformity to the rules of scientific proof. Does God have a desire and a means to guide us into the good? Does God desire to speak salvation and healing to our situations? The colorful mythology about angels to which we are heir is faith's way of answering yes to these questions.

What did the angels sing to the shepherds? They sang of glory to God and peace on the earth. Is that something we need to hear? For sure—two thousand years since the song was sung, and there is precious little peace to be found, either within us or among us. When the people who told the story of Christ's birth wanted to communicate the profundity of human transformation it portended, they appealed to our longing for peace. What the child would bring us was something we did not now have: peace on earth.

So, where is it already? It is here and available. We see, though, that we have become addicted to strife, that we have come to fashion our lives around it, have invited it to stay. We are so loud in our "unpeace," so busy at it, find it so absorbing, that we cannot hear the angel's song. Like some kindergarten teachers who use the device of speaking very softly so that the children will quiet down and listen, the angels sing their song quietly. We will not hear unless we stop and listen.

December 31

Peace on earth and mercy mild,
God and sinners reconciled!

CHARLES WESLEY (1707–1788), HYMN 87

For years, we had a lovely, big New Year's Eve party with a group of old friends. They would arrive at 9:00 in the evening, dinner would be served around 9:30, and the night would end with a champagne toast at midnight. A few years ago, though, we realized we are just too old to do this anymore—we just can't stay up that late. Now we have the party late in the afternoon on New Year's Day instead.

We don't see a lot of those people very often. Some of them we see only at this event, just once a year. So we have a fair amount of catching up to do. People's children have left home—or returned. Other people have retired. This year's party will be the first one without Beverly—she died this past February.

People swarm all over the house at dinner. The younger ones seem to congregate on the stairs. I wish that years ago I had started taking pictures of them eating dinner on the stairs. It would be fun to have a record of that group growing up. Awkward little girls have become beautiful, poised young women in what seems like no time at all. Skinny little boys have deep voices, beards, and mustaches now, and other places to go when they leave the party. Their parents look much the same to me as they always have—maybe a little more gray hair. But time has passed. We are older.

Usually there is a gimmick at the party, some kind of game or costume contest or mock awards ceremony highlighting some aspect of the past year's news that has amused or perplexed us. Most Annoying Public Figure, say, or Most Forgettable Fifteen-Minute Celebrity. One year Dick Young came as Mikhail Gorbachev. That was the same year that Beverly came as A Thousand Points of Light, all wired up with Christmas lights.

The big winners among the gimmicks are usually based on a news event that revealed human sin with painful clarity. Like a lot of satire, ours is irreverent to the point of bad taste and sometimes beyond. If I told you about some of the winning costumes, you'd be offended, so I'll keep them to myself. But in this tomfoolery, we are taking stock of our culture and, therefore, of ourselves. Laughter is a weapon against evil, for political jokes are only funny because they are based on truth, and evil is based on lies.

"I am the way," Jesus said, "and the truth and the life," (John 14:6). Surely the first step in turning from sin is to admit that it's there. Often it is the clown who can admit it first.

January 1 Feast of the Holy Name

Good Christian friends, rejoice with heart and soul and voice;
Now ye need not fear the grave: Jesus Christ was born to save!
Calls you one and calls you all to gain his everlasting hall.
Christ was born to save! Christ was born to save!

JOHN MASON NEALE (1818–1866), HYMN 107

Now, you remember when this hymn was a little different, don't you? We used to insist in this hymn that only the Christian men rejoice on demand, leaving the ladies to consult our own feelings, I suppose. I remember how jarring it was when the new hymnal came out, how like a visitor I felt, singing along from memory as I'd always done and then brought up short by a tweaked pronoun here and there. I remember being relieved that the address of "God Rest You Merry, Gentlemen" was unchanged, although "gentlefolk" would have fit. They did decide to stop claiming, in the final verse, that Christmas "defaced" all other feasts, an overstatement if there ever was one, and further, suggested that we now embrace one another with "Charity" instead of "brotherhood." But "gentlemen" remained. I guess I wasn't the only one who enjoyed the anachronistic experience of that carol.

That was almost twenty years ago. The unanimity of prayer-book and hymnal Episcopalians grew up with has not existed for almost two decades. Except for a society of disgruntled folk who still lobby for its return, we've all gotten used to the new books and settled into enjoyment of texts that include more of us. People who work on this kind of thing, however, know that there's more to be done, and parishes all over the country alter texts to reflect a more inclusive reality in a manner they never would have done before. We'll probably never again define ourselves by a book in the way we used to. Newcomers don't remember anything else, and they don't quite see why anyone would have a problem with that. I guess you kind of had to be there.

It is not easy for the people of God to remember that we define ourselves by the saving action of Jesus Christ and not by anything else. We've always insisted on other things: this or that national allegiance, this or that denomination, this or that credal formulation. But these things don't save us; none of the arrangements we make to live the life of faith are, themselves, the objects of faith, although we sometimes make them so. We don't "believe in" the prayer book or the hymnal, or even in the Bible. We believe in the God they reveal to us.

January 2

Why lies he in such mean estate where ox and ass are feeding?
Good Christian, fear: for sinners here the silent Word is pleading.
WILLIAM CHATTERTON DIX (1837–1898), HYMN 115

We grow up with the idea that a judgment is coming. Christ is the judge, we later learn. Uneasily, we remember everything we've ever heard about hell when we think about what that judgment may be like.

But it's not quite like that. The Word—another name for Christ—is pleading *for* us. In this judgment, it is as if the one who will judge us were also our attorney. God is not hostile or indifferent in the matter of our guilt or innocence. God is on our side. What we have in the last judgment is not justice—if it were, some of us would be in big trouble. What we have instead is mercy. God's desire is to vanquish sin, not to vanquish people. The judgment is carried out wholly within the reality of God's love for us.

Sin is something that gets in between me and God. Whatever it is, and whoever did it, it sits on my heart and takes up space there that would be better given to something more productive. I need to repent and be forgiven, not because I'm afraid of being thrown into a lake of fire, but because my destiny as a beloved child of God is impeded by the roadblocks I have thrown up between us, and my joy will always be incomplete until I am free.

For God, there is no difference between the good and the bad as far as love is concerned. God created them both, and he loves them both. This can be offensive to us, for we need not look far to find grave examples of human cruelty, and it's hard for us to imagine God's love for a cruel person. But God experiences the degradation of the victim and the perpetrator equally, for both are injured in the violence that one has committed and the other has suffered. Both need healing— different kinds of healing, to be sure, but both are in need.

January 3

What can I give him, poor as I am?
If I were a shepherd, I would bring a lamb;
If I were a wise man, I would do my part;
Yet what I can I give him—give my heart.

CHRISTINA ROSSETTI (1830–1894), HYMN 112

"God is so good!" exclaims Clarence as he rounds the corner into the kitchen, carrying an enormous box in both arms. It is full of fruits and vegetables. He has been making the rounds of merchants in the neighborhood all week, collecting fruit and bread and pies and toys and flowers and whatever else people will give him for St. Clement's Christmas celebration. "God is so good!"

Clarence says this all the time. Not everyone who had experienced what Clarence has would think so. He broke his foot a few years back and still has pain with it almost all the time. When he was young, he had to leave his home state in a hurry for having had the temerity to speak directly to a white woman. He has battled his way back into the land of the living from the twin hells of addiction and homelessness. He will never be rich. But Clarence sees the goodness of God everywhere he looks.

God has Clarence's heart. It must be said that Clarence is poor, by any objective measure, but poverty is not what I see when I look at him. Neither does anybody else. "Who is that wonderful man who answers the phone?" a caller often asks me when I come on the line. "Ah, you've experienced Clarence," I say. I walk with him down the street; every third person greets him, as if he were the mayor. He comes back in the afternoon after fetching the children from school and bringing them to the church; at my desk, I hear their voices in the hallway like flutes, telling him about how their day was, and I hear his reassuring voice answer them. He is the grandfather of the after-school.

That's what it's like when God has a person's heart. Small things delight him. He never has so little that he is unwilling to share. Why does a man who has so little live so richly? I guess it must be because God is good.

January 4

And every stone shall cry, in praises of the Child,
By whose descent among us the worlds are reconciled.
Richard Wilbur (b. 1921), Hymn 104

In heaven, everything is perfect—unlike here, where things are usually something of a mess and sometimes really awful. In heaven there is no need. We have paved its streets with gold in our imaginations, and anthropomorphized its residents so that we can have some way of envisioning its reality, but the fact is that the larger world in which God lives is unimaginable to us and will stay that way as long as we are here. It is too different. We don't know the language. The two worlds are irreconcilable.

But Christ reconciles them. Truly human and truly divine, an impossible thing made possible by God. In the first few centuries of our history, some very bright people spent a lot of time and ink trying to spell out just how this was so.

They finally gave up toward the end of the fourth century; our creeds today are strings of their propositions, drained of most of their meaning by centuries of repetition.

I don't care that I can't define Christ's nature. I don't expect to, and I'm not sure I would be better off if I could. I can't even define my husband's nature, and he's sitting right here beside me reading a book. Since when was such definition necessary to love? Even human love is a mystery—the union between two members of the same species—and it rarely makes any sense at all. Plainly, we're in the wrong pew if what we want is things that make sense.

So I don't understand who Jesus is and I don't understand who my husband is. Perhaps it is even the Jesus in my husband that I don't understand, that ineffable something that makes him more than just the sum of his life experience, heredity, and biochemistry. It is the spirit that is always just out of reach, always just beyond the understanding, never reducible to mere thought.

January 5

Be near me, Lord Jesus; I ask thee to stay
Close by me for ever, and love me I pray.
Bless all the dear children in thy tender care,
And fit us for heaven to live with thee there.

TRADITIONAL CAROL, HYMN 101

I had a message from my brother Dave on my machine when I found out that he had died. "I'll be out tonight. I thought you might want to call me tomorrow and find out what's goin' on with me." I didn't get the message; was out of town, didn't pick up my messages, and then he was dead.

My machine is the kind that saves your messages for thirty days and then erases them. "Message saved for... thirty... days," says the artificial voice on the machine. "Message saved for... twenty-one... days." I played it now and then in the weeks that followed his death. I thought idly that maybe I could tape-record it off the machine. "Message saved for... five... days." And then he was gone.

That he loved baseball and model trains. That he was tender with cats and with people, even though he was loud and gruff. That he was angry and I didn't always know why. That he was brave in the face of debilitating illness. These are things I knew about Dave. What do I know now? From his pastor, I learned that he had come to believe in God at the end of his life, after decades of cheerful agnosticism. That he approached death with a spirit of peace. I like knowing these things. But even if he had not come closer to God in life, nothing would have been lost to him in death. If we are not fit for heaven when we leave here, God can make us so by the time we get there. God was no farther away from Dave in the years before Dave felt his presence. God doesn't love those who have trouble believing any less than he loves believers. Sometimes a person will come to me with this fear: that someone he or she loves will be lost in death because he or she is not a Christian. I don't think so. God is larger than any confessional fence that we or our ancestors might have chosen to erect.

Dave loved Christmas when we were little. Packing up his apartment, we found our old nativity set from way back then, packed away in his closet. He hadn't felt well enough to put it up this season, I guess. But he had kept it all those years. He was never far from the kingdom of God.

January 6   Feast of the Epiphany

Vainly we offer each ample oblation,
Vainly with gifts would his favor secure,
Richer by far is the heart's adoration,
Dearer to God are the prayers of the poor.
REGINALD HEBER (1783–1826), HYMN 117

"Will there be any naming opportunities in the renovation of the building?" the consultant for our capital campaign asks. Naming opportunities? Well, could we name our new chapel after a donor if one appeared? How about the sanctuary itself? The parish hall already has a name; if someone came along with more money than Troels Warming had, would we take down his plaque and put up hers? "Given to the glory of God and in loving memory of so-and-so." Sorry, Troels, but business is business.

The glory of God and human memory. God's glory can actually take care of itself, of course. We add nothing to it by any action of ours. Any gift we might offer is only a return to the giver, for we have nothing that did not come from God. The glory of God in the world is shown forth by men and women in a very specific way: God is glorified by us when we serve those in need. Human love expressed in a climate of human dignity glorifies God, wherever and whenever it occurs. Whether it is in a Christian setting or a secular one.

But the giving of conspicuous gifts, even the naming of them after the donor, the affixing of brass plaques to them—these are not evil things. They tell the world that the earth is God's, that the reality of God lives in the midst of all our greed and cynicism. It's a cinch that those in whose memory gifts are given are beyond concern with earthly fame; theirs is another kind of life. Perhaps some of what they couldn't take with them has gone to make the world a better or more beautiful place; that, too, is a sign of God's love. And perhaps their memory helps us in another way. Long after they are just names to us, after anyone who knew them has been dead for years, they remind us that we keep nothing for ourselves anyway, that everything we have has always been God's. So we can learn, even from the very rich, even from those who may not have known it, how to hold what we have lightly.